UMBRELLA DYNASTY PUBLISHING

POEMS FROM THE HEART

BEAUTY IS FELT, SEEN & HEARD

SHACQUAN ROBINSON

POEMS FROM THE HEART

SHACQUAN C. ROBINSON

Poems From The Heart

Copyright 2023

Shacquan Robinson / Umbrella Dynasty Publishing

All rights reserved.

No part of this publication may be reproduced, distributed, or transmitted in any form or by any means, including photocopying, recording, or other electronic or mechanical methods, without the prior written consent of the author, except in the case of brief quotations embodied in critical reviews and certain other noncommercial uses permitted by copyright law. For permission requests, please write to the author at the email address below.

Edited and arranged by Shacquan Robinson & Natalia S.M Aldea

theumbrellax@gmail.com

Umbrella Dynasty Publishing

DEDICATED TO

MA DUKES and
The One Who Only Exist In My Heart

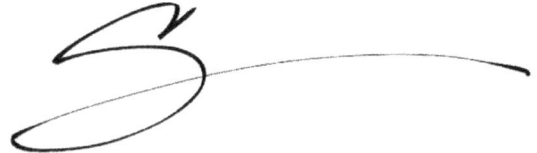

Table Of Contents

DEDICATED TO
Table Of Contents
INTRODUCTION
Poems From The Heart
    Protect Real Men
    Appreciation For My Mother
    Poem For My Momma
    CRYSTAL
    Questions
    Excuse Me
    Toxic Soul
    5
    Cherish Over Cheering
    The Future
    If I Erase Her Pain
    It Happened
    Us
    Won't Leave You
    You Have My Heart
    Hurt
    Do I Really Love You?
    Cherished
    Love
    Why Her?
    Struggles
    Moonlight Smiles pt. 1
    Moonlight Smiles pt. 2

- Dear…
- I Do
- Thoughts of You
- Betrayed
- I Miss You
- That I Love You
- Changes
- Return
- Her Walk
- Lost
- Finding The Way
- Left Me Broken
- Only If
- Someone I Used To Know
- Promises To Keep
- My Love
- I Am
- Broken Heart
- Bestfriend
- So?
- Pain
- She Was
- 9
- I Will
- Strength
- Success
- I Don't Know
- Infinite Love Interest
- What Are We?
- Purpose
- Never Met
- By Myself

THANK YOU

INTRODUCTION

Life has a funny way of expressing itself. Be it through art, music, war or death. Every moment we must cherish it. Because every moment could be the last moment.

I've always looked at things a little different from the next man or woman, as some of you know from my past titles. But rather than living a life in perpetual circumstances, I've decided to live in pure peace. Writing takes me away from the world's events and my own personal events.

Take a look into this book and discover the beauty of words that'll put you in a different place.

Beauty is better seen, felt and heard.

Poems From The Heart

Protect Real Men

as a man today, you're judged by your feats placed against the bet
be them small or big, standards have to be met
we step outside appearing to be powerful & strong
showing the people around us that we do no wrong
walking on eggshells is something i can't do
i walk with conviction, strength in my words so should you
raised by a village, success is what i strive for
whatever it takes, i'll make sure my legacy receives more
take a look into my mind, you'll remain confused
what you see in front of you is a man that can't be used

- Shacquan Robinson, Written November 1, 2022 at 6:35 pm

Appreciation For My Mother

Staying strong, ever since the day you took your last breath
I Understand why you worked so hard even up until your death
But I'm losing faith, shit is getting harder that's what I see
Should I stop here and let this pain take over me
I'm pretty sure that's not what you want, trust me I do
Your first born, morally respected, just like you
They're telling me go ahead and cry, just give it all up
Demons lie, so do people. Please shut the fuck up
I still feel you, even when I sleep hoping you come home
A pain inside that I use to become hard as a stone
Yvette tatted on my neck motivation on a daily basis
But then I turn into the mirror why do I seem so faceless
Doesn't matter I'll keep on pushing I got the dynasty
The leader that you made me today but this is not a fantasy
Here's another for your appreciation from the living life
See you soon, imma keep the peace, opposite of strife

- Shacquan Robinson, written June 5, 2022 at 4:36am

Poem For My Momma

You were the **A**ngel that kept us straight
The **B**eauty in our lives
Always giving us **C**onfidence to do more
Determined to make sure we were good
Educated us on how to live
Family was your number 1 priority
A **G**oddess you was
Humbleness is something no one could take from you
Of course you was **I**ntelligent and **I**rreplaceable
Jolly by nature
One of a **K**ind
Loving nature elevated us
Mean in your own way but extremely **M**eaningful to us
Nurturing from day 1
Too **O**ptimistic and always **O**vercame your struggles
The **P**arent every child should praise
Qualities that could not be matched
Extremely **R**espected and **R**enowned
You showed us your **S**trength in tough situations
Tough. Nothing **T**imid about you
A **U**nique style of love and care
Our most **V**aluable treasure
The 1st teacher, instilling us with your **W**isdom
e**X**quisite
Our loving old lady in our eyes, but **Y**outhful in our hearts
Zealful, and with that enthusiasm we will make your dreams come true

These are the **ABC**s of You

MA, YOU WILL BE MISSED. WE LOVE YOU

November 13, 1973 - December 9, 2017

- Shacquan Robinson,

written April 14, 2018 at 3:07am

CRYSTAL CLEAR

Have you ever needed something so bad you didn't know what to do
But then you found it and it's like you always knew
Walking through life playing the game how you want
So that a win is guaranteed, not putting up a front
Since you dropped in I knew my plan
Get her on board, make me a new man
A wife is chosen, a man is made
I've made myself that man, i can't be swayed
After years of trial and error, it's nothing new
None of it is complete until she says "I do"
I finally understand now, it's crystal clear
You said you were scared, baby I choose you, there is nothing to fear

- Shacquan Robinson, written January 17, 2023 1:49am

CRYSTAL

Chilling here
Realizing
Y
Sentimental
Thinkers
Always
Love Hard

Now how does a man explain the things he feel without being labeled something soft like some
He shows his love through respect and honor as if it were to his mom
Relationship always made me throw up, causing pain
But when you came around I felt no illness, it kept me sane
I want to give you my mind, I'm competent
To realize this is what I want this is what I like, it's no pretend
A lot of people throw this relationship stuff around like it's a trend
I been around for years but some things I can't amend
I got a voice of reason from the Host high and my boys down here
They all tell me it takes time, when you want something that's dear
To the heart, they say
it'll make its way
Every other girl I found it hard to stay
Lots of trauma you went through, I can feel that
But imagine through my eyes all the pain I've met
Developed a mindset

to keep me fighting it,
it's true
But when I first heard your voice I just thought of you saying "I do"

- Shacquan Robinson, written January 17, 2023 5:04am

Questions

Sitting and thinking, sitting and writing
One messed up night got my girl questioning what's happening
I told my problem, it's hard to understand
Not speaking on the questions I have, haunted by just being a man
She questions the validity of the stories I present
I'm tired of bringing them up in every conversation I get
I just want to focus on something I prayed for
I'm tired of living the way I did, something that you'll call a man whore
I found a good thing proverbs 18:22
I'm not gonna fuck this up between me and you
Once I'm invested I'm going all in
Baby Im not tryna stay a friend, but rather be your husband

- Shacquan Robinson, written January 25, 2023 4:16

Excuse Me

Excuse me miss can I speak to you
You took my interest when you walked through
Just wondering if you had a man
If not, so what's your plan
You stepping through here looking like you're choosing
I just want an opportunity to show you what I'm using
This isn't a game no ma'am this isn't a front
I wanna show you something different, sorry if I'm coming off too blunt
I just like what I see and I'm straight to the point
Not wasting your time or tryna to exploit
An issue I see with you around here, how's this sound
Let me be the man around your arm, no more clowns

- Shacquan Robinson,
written February 19, 2023 at 6:00am

Toxic Soul

You let me lose track of time, you let me taste your toxic soul
you brought frustration in my life
a toxic pain inserted like a dirty knife
now the bloods coming out of this toxic hole
step right inside show up bitch
I didn't die put you got me in this ditch
You let me lose track of time, you let me taste your toxic soul
how must I move on when you have full control
toxic air, toxic atmosphere, you're supposed to be the one I console
did you become a narcissist when you met me
Or was this something from jump street
A toxic scent I wish weren't true
it lingers in your laughter, I hope it's not really you
Given all the pain we faced together and apart
no way I'll let you taint my heart
You let me lose track of time, You let me taste you toxic soul
To be what we all think we should, a man of confidence I shall become
your life is done in my book, close the chapter leaving you numb

- Shacquan Robinson,
written February 20, 2023 @ 4:46am

5

4 had good and bad times
I showed you how much I cared, showed you're mines
You said you never had something before
I gave you just a little more
More family you was introduced to
They said you're special, you said I'm special to you
This is a new round I'm ready to give
4 in the books 5th is to be relieved
A positive journey together we're walking in
But that's the definition of a twin
Flame, or whatever you want to call it
We're going to let everyone know how we commit
To something we both asked for with Nothing to negotiate
We don't have to do anything that we're both gonna hate
I want you by my side that's definitely something respected
Running fast to the finish line but there's no exit
No matter where we are in the universe
I'll continue to look into your eyes to escape the worse
So again cheers to another month
My future, my soul, my wife I love who you are so much

- Shacquan Robinson,
written March 1, 2023 @ 5:18am

Cherish Over Cheering

Doesn't matter how many accolades I collect,
the money I make or the stories I write.

My greatest accomplishment is having the ability
to please you and cherish you

- Shacquan Robinson,
written March 17, 2023 @ 5:32pm

The Future

I wish we could speed up this thing we call life because knowing the future but not being able to experience it is more painful than being in the present with the unknown.

I just want to see the future of us together...

- Shacquan Robinson,
written March 17, 2023 @ 4:44am

If I Erase Her Pain

If I erase her pain
Will she do the same
Singing by the moon
I loved you too soon
Tell the truth about me babe

Marry me
Join me
I need you to see
Will she throw us away

So if I erase her pain
Will she do the same

I asked myself this daily
Yet I couldn't see it clearly
So if she left me today
She in fact erased my pain
Cuz with her near me
I understood she's what kept me insane

- Shacquan Robinson,
written March 20, 2023 @ 7:45am

It Happened

I said it once and it felt right since then
February 4th is when I felt the win
I told you those 3 words that many run from
But I know for a fact that us 2 would feel numb
Just looking for the 1 that would not play me
Now she's stuck in my mind, she's all I see
Writing this cuz on our 4th I spoke I love you
1 month after and it's still the same nothing new
Not gonna break your heart it's mine to cherish
A crush turned into love and it'll never perish
Shout out to your parents
for not knowing they made me happy
Now you're here just making me cocky
My girl educated, sexy and athletic
Funny, loving and cold hearted
Won't trade her for the others I seen
They don't touch my heart like my queen
My peace my sanity my bully
I'm opening to you fully
I love you smiley
Hopefully it's the same baby

- Shacquan Robinson,
written March 7, 2023 @ 5:55am

Us

I don't care what we go through
You put your lips on mine
You put your arms around me
We touch hands
On a daily basis
Even if it's for a second.
Cuz we are pushing for the long term
And regardless of our attitudes we are us first

- Shacquan Robinson,
written March 20, 2023 @ 7:53am

Won't Leave You

Shit hurts

This shit hurts so bad
Why are you always getting so mad
When you're the one that brought this shit
Hanging out with your hoe friends doing dumb shit

All I wanted was my own family
You're showing that's not the vision for me
I really don't know what to do though
Laying on my back like a nympho
Used and abused getting fucked around
Come on baby don't do this to us right now

Why are you putting me out of your heart yo
You just told me it's just us though
Why you stressing me out leaving me cold and numb
When you're the one I need real love from

This shit hurts

- Shacquan Robinson, written April 8, 2023 @ 2:27am

You Have My Heart

I don't like when you're away
Everyday, I rather wake up to your face
Not a day goes by where you're forgotten about
Even when I close my eyes I know there's no doubt
That the love I have for you is definitely real
This is something I want us to continue to feel
Please get the picture that this isn't a game
You are the one that strikes my brain

You have my heart

No one can tell me that this is wrong
Because I did what I wanted for this long
And now that you've stepped in
I'm working towards something that should've already been
A family that you and I can develop
I'm feeling you and my love is enveloped
In hopes of joy and a future, in our center
Let's make our 6th something to remember

You have my heart

- Shacquan Robinson,
written April 18, 2023 @ 5:36pm

Hurt

Times have changed but not my heart
I've loved every moment that you've given me from the start
From the first time you said hello, to our final goodbye
But now when I go out all I can do is cry
I try so hard to move on from you
But my confidence is low I don't know what to do
Rejection from others cuz they see the weakness in me
Since you've left I've been so empty
I followed you on IG from a secret account
You look so happy that's without a doubt
But yes times have changed but not my heart
I can't seem to shake this pain since we've been apart

- Shacquan Robinson, written May 9, 2023 @ 5:24am

Do I Really Love You?

I wake up and sleep everyday, always thinking about us and our future. You say you're an over-thinker but I over think more from you constantly saying that you believe you're not on my level and I could do better. But if I wanted better I'll find a way to clone you and have 1 more. I believe everyday we will get better at our joint lives rather than separated apart. In the mists of it all I like to see you do your thing. It's something that makes me proud of you. Easy for me to say, "that's my lady". No hesitation because I'm happy now. So yes, I do believe I love you, because no other person on the planet has the amount of energy that I have to give unto you...

- Shacquan Robinson, written May 23, 2023 @ 5:42pm

Cherished

For my past you made me forget
For my present you made it a gift
For my future it's no longer a myth

You are cherished

- Shacquan Robinson,
written May 21, 2023 @ 10:13pm

Love

Love is like a rose, Beautiful and sweet.
It fills our hearts with joy, And makes our lives complete.
Love is a feeling that's hard to describe,
It fills us with warmth and makes our hearts come alive.
It's a bond that connects us, through good times and bad,
it's something we cherish, forever if it's ever had.

Love is like river, flowing endlessly,
It's a force of nature, that's as strong as can be.
The feeling that's shared, between a heart and another heart,
something that should never, ever depart

Love is a journey, that takes us through life,
It's an adventure that's filled with joy and strife.
It's a treasure that's found, in the depths of the soul,
And it's something that makes you, me and the rest of us, truly feel whole.

- Shacquan Robinson,
written June 6, 2023 @ 6:20am

Why Her?

Cause I read her eyes

She's been through so much and I'm so proud that she made it this far. She didn't deserve the bad things that happened to her. Since she went through the struggles then and now, as her man I'm willing to go through them today. Even though she needs an escape, I'm lost in her eyes as she is mine. I seen her journey and I'm stuck on that route. I will not leave her stranded like the souls before. It may hurt inside but her smile shows something different. I want to make her a future mother, and a loving wife, that's my mission.

I am her keeper and those are my whys

- Shacquan Robinson, written June 5, 2023 @ 6:18am

Struggles

Water will seep through of a torn roof
But if the foundation is strong.
The shakes and the earthquakes will not bring the house apart
It's gonna rain, but our job together is to make sure we keep our heads right.

I love you like no other
I still want us…

- Shacquan Robinson,
written June 5, 2023 @ 5:54pm

Moonlight Smiles pt. 1

I miss the passion that we once shared
i miss the smiles that resembled the moonlight
on dark nights

- Shacquan Robinson,
written June 3, 2023 @ 7:56pm

Moonlight Smiles pt. 2

I miss the passion that we once shared
i miss the smiles that resembled the moonlight
on dark nights

There come a time where struggles beat us
But through it all it was nothing that would make me cuss
Scream, Fight or Disrespect my Queen
The mother of my 1st born and the woman of my dreams
I wanted to leave the painful conversations and kiss you
by any means

So i say to you this
Please don't let us be the ex couple that says we miss
The jokes and the laughs
The kisses and the hugs
The knowledge and the thoughts
Because through all past experiences
I don't want to reminisce
About how much I cared for you
The girl I met one day, that told me "I Do"

Please let's get back to us baby girl

- Shacquan Robinson,
written June 7, 2023 @ 7:28am

Dear...

Dear Mom
Today I didn't give up. Even though it's hurting me more...

Dear Dad
We don't talk much. But you're still the man...

Dear God
I'm sorry for bugging you. I'm just so tired...

- Shacquan Robinson, written June 13, 2023 @ 7:45pm

I Do

I am still
Silently hoping that time will
Give us Hopes and Dreams
Give us Mistakes and Struggles
Joy and Laughter
In which every moment
We continue to find the hearts
We had on the day we both said
I do

- Shacquan Robinson,
written June 16, 2023 @ 4:50am

Thoughts of You

I built dreams around you
I was willing to change my life for you
Somewhere in time, I was the one that wouldn't hide you
It's hard to quit you
Because I can still smell you
I can still feel you
I was a special person that was made for you
Why did you show me a different you
The character before was the better version of you
Please return to you
The end was supposed to be me and you

- Shacquan Robinson,
written June 14, 2023 @ 10:00am

Betrayed

As I lay in bed
Staring into the ceiling
I feel the last time you laid on my chest
That was the day I felt the best
You made me feel good on my bday even without the sex
Cuz that was the last thing on our mine compared to the rest
Of the world who only have that to offer
But we was so good, we were getting stronger
We talked about marriage and not just a wedding
Cuz love was in our future, I knew where we was heading
Why did you betray us now I can't think
Our connection was broken, what happened to the link
You damaged me badly
And i was supposed to be the one you hold sincerely
I'm respected feared and honored by the people of this world
But when I came home I wanted you to hold my vulnerable side that was curled
I can't see nothing past this now
Because every girl that gives me a smile, I still look down
Because their smile isn't my child's mother
And I don't want no other

- Shacquan Robinson,
written June 14, 2023 @ 7:11am

I Miss You

When they ask me about you
I hold back my emotions because the memories are too beautiful
But I gotta live with a lie
Cuz I'm too embarrassed to cry
You might not have told them about us
But the people in my world knew without a fuss
That crystal crook was my woman
The woman that this year I was gonna take her hand
I was to Look into her eyes and say marry me
Not for your looks not for your body
But for your laugh your mind your energy that made me happy
I was so proud to claim you
I hope one day you know
That when they say where is Dre,
You lie to them too because we weren't supposed to go astray
it's true what they say
Our story didn't have an happy ending,
but it had a happy middle and beginning
I'm tearing up as I write this poem
Remembering you will now be a part of my norm...

I miss you...

- Shacquan Robinson,
written June 14, 2023 @ 6:57am

That I Love You

I hope when you wake up to start your day baby
You remember how you said you couldn't sleep next to another man other than me

I made you smile
I made you feel loved
I made you feel safe

But I want you to know when I wake up
I still think about kissing your soft lips and squeezing your butt
You are on my Mind the woman I was to court
But this is why my sleep has been short
I'm not at peace anymore, my life has changed for the worse

I need you here. Me laying next to you.
Please Text me when you have the chance so I can tell you
That I rather be with you!

I fucking still Love You

- Shacquan Robinson,
written June 14, 2023 @ 6:35am

Changes

Times have changed but not my heart
I've loved every moment that you've given me from the start
From the first time you said hello, To our final goodbye
But now when I go out I can feel nothing but to cry
I try so hard to move on from you
But my confidence is low I don't know what to do
Rejection from others cuz they see the weakness in me
Since you've left I've been so empty
I followed you on IG from a secret account
You look happy that's without a doubt
But yes times have changed but not my heart
I can't seem to shake this pain since we've been apart

- Shacquan Robinson,
written May 9, 2023 @ 5:24am

Return

At first I was minding my business
Then I seen you walk by
Now I crave your attention
But I hurt when I'm not having it
So I rather return to the day, when I was minding my business

- Shacquan Robinson,
written June 17, 2023 @ 4:38am

Her Walk

She walked with a grace that no woman can beat
This is the girl that I have to meet

She told me her name followed by a smile
Just in that instant I thought to myself how
Can a woman like this be without a man now
She told me without me asking, "constantly I've been let down"

It's been clowns in my life, always doing me wrong!
What do you want from me, a repeated sad love song?
I told her I was different, let me lead the way
Guidance is all I want to offer, you can leave or you can stay

So we made it one year then the craziest shit happened
She walked out my life, instant retraction
Now I'm thinking about her walk, the past one and current
I needed more time, I know she was my soulmate for certain

Now her walk is something I will always remember
She walked in and walked out, it's cold in here but it's not December

- Shacquan Robinson, written June 17, 2023 @4:47am

Lost

You're the only person I'll look for in a crowded room
Remember I texted you I could spot you from a mile or two
You told me you can feel my energy, you don't have to look hard
You was connected to me until you went too far
He got your attention I don't know how
Where did he come from to turn us foul
Were lost in connection now we can't fix shit
Guess you betrayed me for a quick fix
Now we're stuck torn between love and hurt
I don't even feel my heartbeat and I'm not even in the dirt
I wish you would've just told me the problem baby
All my promises was kept, yours was maybe
Now that we're lost, no one knows what to do
You still love me and I still love you

- Shacquan Robinson, written June 17, 2023 @ 5:02am

Finding The Way

It's definitely the look in my eyes when I see you smile
That's because in your eyes time moves slow on the dial
But at night I wish my pillow was yours to lay your head
Wishing I wouldn't have to send poems that you read
You can just stand over me and watch me write
I knew having you was finding the way, and now I'm right
Let's try and do this better we're so close
Moving higher on the mountain don't let go of the rope
The day my heart skipped a beat I thought long and hard
No change is bad so with you around I can change with no regard
For thinking of negative possibilities
So I'm asking is finding the way better opportunities

- Shacquan Robinson, written June 17, 2023 @ 5:59am

Left Me Broken

I know we could've been great
U wasn't ready to go steady but it was fate
Showing you love I forgot myself
Couldn't see how damaged you was but what else
Wish we got pregnant, a son
That would guarantee me more time with u
I can't blame u ma
As I pray for you, you still let demons in
I was guidance but peer pressure was your sin
I guess it's the stars unaligned
That's why your energy declined
You said "i do and I meant that shit"
After that I got rid of all my mistresses
Months later you gave your womb to another man
When this was the year to take my hand
Into marriage, we were one
Can't believe now you're done
You did it on my birthday month
Evil desires turned you into a slut
So baby, no promises of mine were broken
Your next "truth" will always continue to be destruction

- Shacquan Robinson,
written June 16, 2023 @ 5:08am

Only If

If only I could give you my eyes
Then you would be able to see why I claim you as mines
You made everything seem so calm I instantly had a list of whys

Like

Why did she come into my life
Why does her smile remove all strife
Why does the smell of her scent linger after hours apart
Why does her presence slow down my heart

But

Only if I was able to hold more time
I would trade everything in a drop of a dime
I'm not lucky by a long shot
Blessed is a better term why not
The memories we made can't be erased
Multiple girls in my phone but you can't be replaced

Only if you love me the same

- Shacquan Robinson,
written June 21, 2023 @ 3:46am

Someone I Used To Know

She had a smile of a goddess
The one that lights up a dark mind
You could be going through tough times
But her gaze up at you will make it all go away
She was going through her own shit but her hugs will correct all doubts
Her spirit alone will make a good man become better

That's the someone I used to know

But now her gaze isn't on you
It's been tainted by another person or two
Her environment killed the good girl she once was
She let go of your hand and led herself away
Into the darkness she wanted to run from
Now she's screaming out for help
Saying no one loves her
But it only comes from alcohol and drugs

That's the new someone I know

But you're still waiting for her
Hoping and praying she sees your energy through all the fog
Reconnect to you so you both can be happy again
Plan the life y'all seen a future within
As long as it takes til she comes back and becomes

Someone I used to know

- Shacquan Robinson,
written June 25, 2023 @ 7:38pm

Promises To Keep

I made promises that I have to keep
Because I would never walk away from from something this deep

You said you were done but we tried another day
You broke it off again
And we were right back in each others face

When I said I'll leave
You said no you're not
You was hurt and came to see me that day
So we talked about a lot

We're back together, gonna try this once more
But time away makes our hearts sore
You say I'm your man and this what you want
We know each other too much to put up a front

We can't let each other go let's call it what it is
You're mine and I'm yours til the very end

But i made promises that I have to keep
Because if I were you i wouldn't walk away from me

- Shacquan Robinson,
written June 22, 2023 @ 8:16pm

My Love

I knew my love didn't vanish
When you said what you did
And I still looked for the good in you
The innocence I've seen in your eyes
The little girl who smiled hard
The adult that tries to stay happy
I want to see that again
That's how I knew my love didn't vanish

- Shacquan Robinson,
written July 3, 2023 @ 5:41am

I Am

In whispered moments, a gentle breeze,
Resides the power to set us a-free,
A tapestry woven of thoughts profound,
Affirmations, their magic unbound.

I am the architect of my own fate,
I am the creator of my dreams, both small and great,
With every word that I choose to speak,
I mold my reality, both strong and meek.

I am worthy, deserving of love's embrace,
I am A vessel of light, filled with boundless grace,
In each step I take, I find strength anew,
For within me, a universe blooms and grew.

I am courageous, unafraid to soar,
To explore the depths, where dreams implore,
With wings unfurled, I dance upon the wind,
Embracing the unknown, where new beginnings begin.

I am resilient, a warrior of the soul,
Through trials and tribulations, I am whole,
With unwavering belief, I rise above,
Transforming challenges into acts of love.

I am abundant, blessed with endless wealth,
Not merely measured by material stealth,
For gratitude's embrace fills my heart's core,
And prosperity flows, forevermore.

I am a beacon, shining bright and clear,
Illuminating paths, dispelling fear,
With compassion as my guide, I lead the way,
Touching lives, imparting hope each passing day.

So let us speak with words of love and might,
Affirm our dreams, and embrace the light,
For in the realm of possibilities untold,
Affirmations breathe life, as dreams unfold.

- Shacquan Robinson,
written July 4, 2023 @ 4:20am

Broken Heart

In the silence of a shattered heart,
Lies a tale of love torn apart,
A symphony that once played so bright,
Now whispers in the shadowed night.

Underneath the moon's soft glow,
I hear Echoes of laughter we used to know,
In the remnants of a sweet, love song,
A broken heart feels so fucking wrong.

Flickers of memories, like stars in the night,
Remember to poem about your smile being so bright,
But each thought of recollection brings me pain,
Like a summer storm, never got to kiss in the rain.

A heart once full, now a chasm deep,
Where secrets of lost love weep,
My mission was strong, now a mission failed vastly,
if this was a love movie, I'll play the only part so cast me

my silence sings a mournful tune,
A song for a love but my heart is doomed ,
Yet within these ruins of despair,
A tender resilience starts to flare.

A broken heart, yet not destroyed,
In the void, finds a new void,
With every beat, it starts to mend,
Then someone says your name, and it's broken again.

For my heart that's broken is still alive,
In its fragments, it learns to thrive.
It learns to cope with pain and guilt
In the wreckage, turned off the road with a bad tilt

So, fear not this broken heart,
It's but a canvas for life's art.
In its breaking, it finds its part,
It's in the mending, love will never restart.

- Shacquan Robinson,
written July 8, 2023 @ 4:36am

Bestfriend

From the first day I said hi,
to the day I asked if you were single
Not a day has gone by
That I don't hear bells, like a Christmas or wedding jingle
You made everything important even during our rough times in this shit
But we made it through, we definitely conquered it
Getting closer to a year since you came in & I told u I don't do female friends
either you're my girl, my business partner or a fuck friend
U instantly took the title as the lady in my life
We learned a lot about each other and even took time apart to figure out if this was right
But today I can say strongly that you have become the best friend I needed
You came in & changed my outlook, 100% succeeded
I appreciate you so much smiley
You're the one that I was supposed to meet finally
Continue to help me become better man
And imma continue to do all I can

- Shacquan Robinson, written July 20, 2023 @ 2:48am

So?

So it's finally over, You showed your true colors
Never would've thought that your smiles was fake
I really needed them to make me feel great
Needed them to feel important
But tonight it cut me deep
When you said that I don't really meet
The expectations you have and you think it's forced
All I ever showed was that I needed just a touch
A touch of your love so I can complete my mission
Everything is a burden to me but you're what's missing
So I finally realized this 4 letter word wasn't meant for me to have
It was just something I was supposed to give like my last
I learned my lesson I was supposed to be broken
It's all gone now thanks to your choices
I'm sorry I'm not who you really wanted
So now I know I have to live broken hearted

- Shacquan Robinson,
written July 23, 2023 @ 1:16am

Pain

It's coming from the heart A pain I've felt before
But with u doing it to me I feel like I can't take anymore
We are good for each other I know this for a fact
But you don't look at me the same and I can see that
I'm hurting right now writing this stupid love poem
Cuz you was my inspiration, a person I really longed for
But now the pain has taken over my body
The shakes are starting again
I wouldn't even care if tonight it all had to end
By that line I mean my life I'm living now
Cuz if you're not included it's really no need for a smile
I tried time and time again to make this shit work
I'm tired of different women who don't see my worth
They want me for this they need me for that
But I never met a girl that can keep my spirit in check
But it's fine now I get the picture that's given to me
That bottle of alcohol is really starting to speak to me
Maybe I'll walk over to it and take a little or maybe a lot
Fuck it since you're gone now I'm not gotta take just one shot
So now the pain feels like it's drifting away
It's getting cold in here I'll just close my eyes for today

- Shacquan Robinson,
written July 23, 2023 @ 1:32am

She Was

She was
My Eve to my Adam
My Nefertiti to my Ramesses
My Breseis to my Achilles
My Roxanna to my Alexander
My Gorgo to my Leonidas
My Bonnie to my Clyde
She was
My Rib

- Shacquan Robinson,
written June 15, 2023 @ 12:12am

9

The number of completion
The time where it's all over
It was peace it was war
But it was our journey to conquer
So now we're here
The end of the term
Summer to summer
But not a complete circle
Why did you do that
I just said our other relationships ended selfishly
Yet you gave me that pain again, effortlessly
No stress in my life but you brought it at the end
I'm feeling used and it's nothing i can do
Nine in
but three away
I wanted a family to myself not to be lonely universally

- Shacquan Robinson,
written July 23, 2023 @ 3:17am

I Will

I will stay when it gets hard
I will stay once you get confused
I will stay when things are fun
I will stay when it's all rain and no sun
I will stay if you lose your senses

I won't regret the decision I made to stay

- Shacquan Robinson,
written June 22, 2023 @ 8:57pm

Strength

The strength of one
Can be the strength of all
The the strength of all
Can't be the strength of one
Weakness all around it must be stopped
But if the world believes it's right, that's when you depart
Living in a world where peer pressure can thrive
One must be stern in his mind
Pass the test with aplomb
But don't let the confidence send you to the tomb
Have faith, courage and creed to stand alone
If a challenge comes, let your aura speak of your story, atone
I am what I am, more strength than most
I set my boundaries in my world, for I am the host

- Shacquan Robinson,
written August 1, 2023 @ 7:39pm

Success

In a world where dreams and ambitions meet,
A sacred place beneath the avatar's feet,
A leap of faith, an opportunity to jump, small yet fleet,
The whispering soul of success can be so sweet.

Success, can we all reach it, in an ocean so vast,
An elusive ship, moving fast,
We chase our shadow, our sails, we cast,
With great passion, our troubles surpassed.

Born with dreams, yet sheltered by might,
Nurtured by trials, in the day or the night,
My dreams for growth, unobtainable for some height,
Success, at last, in this generous light.

A journey, winding, neither straight nor clear,
Where courage tangles with encroaching fear,
The distant vision, not out of reach, so very near,
Success is a dance, solo seeing in a clear mirror.

So, dream, of your heart's passion aflame,
Seek not the endgame, nor the fame,
But each moment you struggled well,
For in this is your product, a promise to not fail

- Shacquan Robinson,
written August 11, 2023 @ 5:50am

I Don't Know

I'm Trapped Somewhere Between wanting to forget us
And wanting to hold us
Because there's things I wanted to say
Like the convos I say to myself as if you're here.

I know that we will find each other again like in our past life.
So now I sleep more cuz in my dreams I see your smile more.
In some dreams I see us standing by the water laughing at how we beat everyone that played us.
Then crying cuz we could be apart.

Every song I hear reminds me of you and every silent moment I hear your heart beat.
Those are the days I miss you.
Maybe when the time is right you'll touch me again.
Standing in one place writing this poem someone randomly said your touch deprived.
You're my favorite story I repeat over and over it's the truth
even though the pain is unbearable.

- Shacquan Robinson,
written August 11, 2023 @ 5:59am

Infinite Love Interest

I really miss you right now
Not sexually but spiritually
For you're the person
I chose to be vulnerable with
Now I'm empty
I didn't forget your scent
That I loved the most
Easy separate lives we made one but you're not the same person

Letting you go, I can't
Opposite of what I chose to live, with no rest
Vexed by the time and space you put between us, but
Everything reminds me of you

I never will have beef with love, but
Not accepting it if you're not carrying it
That's you I miss right now that I still love right now that
I still want, an
Eternal love that won't fade
Returning one day to start our family
Everyone is confused by how you up and left
Sadly I have to tell them a lie cuz I'm hurting
The world abandoned me, then you followed with them

Proved over and over again that I was going to protect you
Lies I never told just to show you
Endless love, something you asked for and needed
At least I didn't forget our main goal, which was to
Surrender my heart to you so you can hold it
Erased all my past, easy to forget

Closing in on that very first day, when you
Opened my eyes to true peace
Making me feel like I could take on the world even more
Every day made me feel invincible

Hope you take this in
Opening our communication again
Marrying you, starting our journey anew
Every cell in me craves you

- Shacquan Robinson,
written September 21, 2023 @
7:08am

What Are We?

I thought that we, we're right for me
The missing link, the missing puzzle piece
But Now I see
I told my truth
Before I met you, jinxed like a damn fool
Because I said "after you
There would be nothing left to do"
The void was filled with you in it
now it's back
But I can't sleep around knowing it
Was supposed to be you and Shac
Quan to the end
But I wasn't clear on which end was meant
I thought god knew it
But I was wrong about shit
The end of time, not the journey
I wanted eternity
Now what are we
A question I ask myself because you're not in front of me

- Shacquan Robinson,
written September 29, 2023 @ 7:20am

Purpose

For quite some time
I knew I had a purpose
Then you walked towards me
That's when I knew I added another objective

- Shacquan Robinson,
written October 14, 2023 @ 10:16am

Never Met

I've never met a person
That understood me from day one
Until I met you
The only one that spoke my language

- Shacquan Robinson,
written January 28, 2024 at 5:50am

By Myself

Being alone is nothing to me
But when you stepped in with destiny
You were the one you see
Because since that day
I only enjoyed your company

- Shacquan Robinson,
written January 28, 2024 at 6:06am

THANK YOU

Thank you for continuing to support me. These poems were written by me throughout the year and are placed in most of my books. I wanted to share a skill and talent that my dad, Charlie T. Morring passed down to me. That man was very skilled with his words with women and knowing how to express himself through poetry. Even writing lots of poems for my mom.

Thanks for enjoying this writing journey with me. Thanks for all the love and support throughout the years

I love you all

UD3M

www.ingramcontent.com/pod-product-compliance
Lightning Source LLC
Chambersburg PA
CBHW031455040426
42444CB00007B/1118